Copyright © 2025 by Elizabeth Haidle

Tundra Books, an imprint of Tundra Book Group,
a division of Penguin Random House of Canada Limited

All rights reserved. The use of any part of this publication reproduced, transmitted in any form or by any means, electronic, mechanical, photocopying, recording, or otherwise, or stored in a retrieval system, without the prior written consent of the publisher — or, in case of photocopying or other reprographic copying, a license from the Canadian Copyright Licensing Agency — is an infringement of the copyright law.

Please note that no part of this book may be used or reproduced in any manner for the purpose of training artificial intelligence technologies or systems.

Library and Archives Canada Cataloguing in Publication

Title: Drawing is... / Elizabeth Haidle.
Names: Haidle, Elizabeth, 1974- author, illustrator.
Identifiers: Canadiana (print) 20240344111 | Canadiana (ebook) 20240344162 | ISBN 9781774885031 (hardcover) | ISBN 9781774885048 (EPUB)
Subjects: LCSH: Drawing—Technique—Juvenile literature.
Classification: LCC NC730 .H35 2025 | DDC j741.2—dc23

Published simultaneously in the United States of America by
Tundra Books of Northern New York, an imprint of Tundra Book Group,
a division of Penguin Random House of Canada Limited

Library of Congress Control Number: 2024932887

Edited by Kyo Maclear
Designed by John Martz and Elizabeth Haidle
The illustrations in this book were created with pencil, ink, gouache, graphite powder, digital collage and countless cups of caffeinated tea.
The text was hand-lettered by Elizabeth Haidle and set in American Typewriter.

Printed in China

www.penguinrandomhouse.ca

1 2 3 4 5   29 28 27 26 25

DRAWING IS...

by Elizabeth Haidle

YOUR GUIDE TO SCRIBBLED ADVENTURES

tundra

DRAWING IS...

WHAT IS DRAWING?

Drawing is two-dimensional traveling.
You can travel far away.
You can dive inward.

What you create on the paper can be a place for you to inhabit, a home of your own making. A home is different than a house — it is a feeling, a belonging.

In your sketchbook, any page you open to is a place you can explore, think and feel, experiment and question.

Well, what are you waiting for?

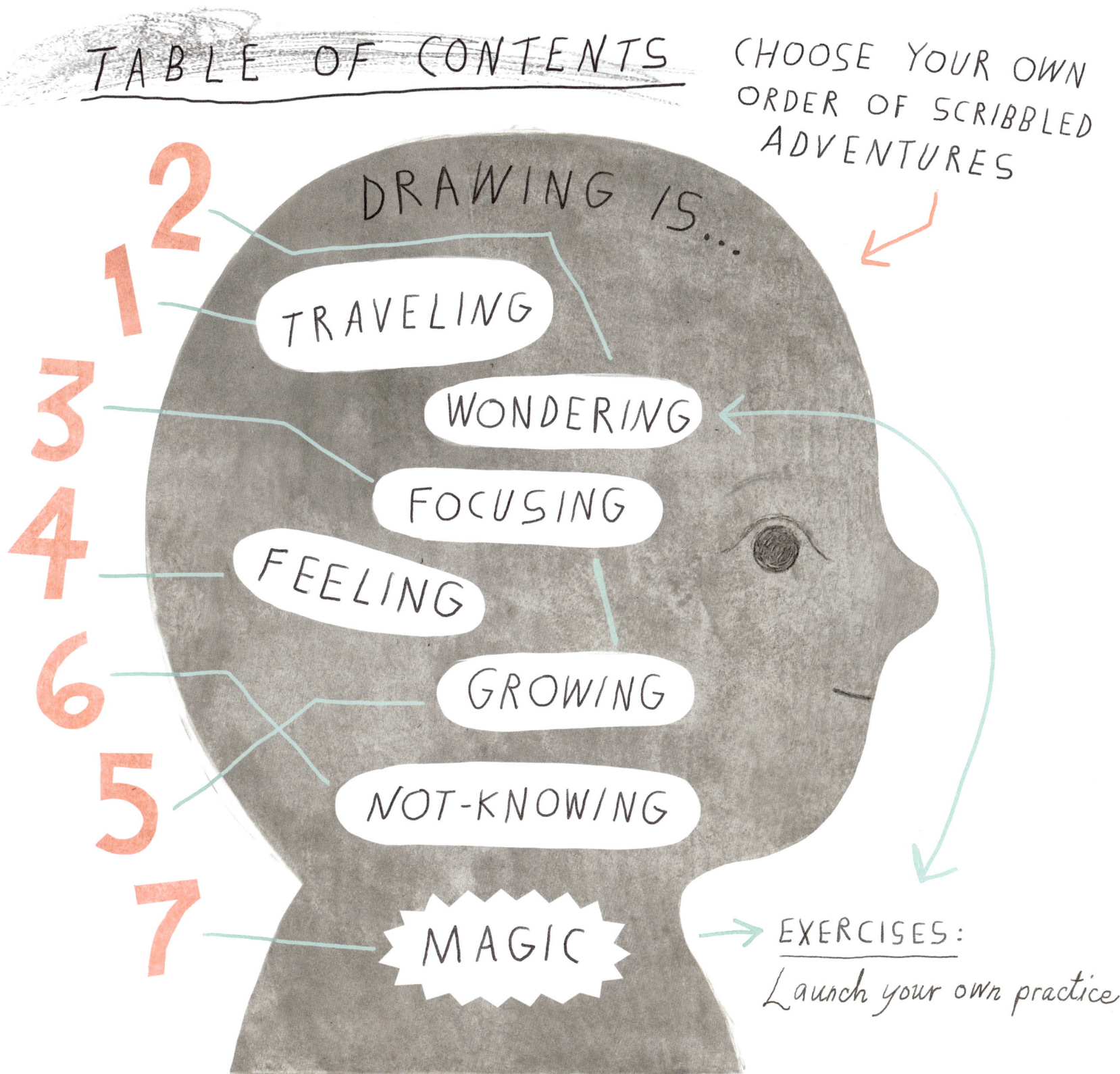

OKAY, SO, DRAWING IS... WAIT!
WHAT IS DRAWING NOT?

Drawing is NOT a contest.

Unless trying is winning and you are the only contestant.

Drawing is NOT just for the "talented ones."

Talent is something people have different amounts of, but it always grows as you practice.

Drawing is NOT exercise.*

You will need to drop the pencil and stretch your body. Your brain resides in your body, so taking care of your body is a way to keep ideas happening.

Drawing is NOT right or wrong.

You are a person. With a point of view. Everything you think, say and do is influenced by who you are. You have artistic freedom to draw things in whatever way suits you.

Drawing is NOT a waste of time.

Time is something we either use for a purpose, or spend on distractions — letting something else dictate our attention. Drawing is always a choice... even if you draw distractedly! Artists often dive into their sketchbooks to take their mind off other things.

*Unless you are at the shore, with a long stick in your hand, carving gigantic lines in the wet sand as you move. Which I recommend trying because the waves rush in like a massive eraser, wiping it all away. This can be very freeing.

NOW, DO YOU HAVE WHAT IT TAKES TO DRAW?
TAKE THIS QUICK QUESTIONNAIRE:

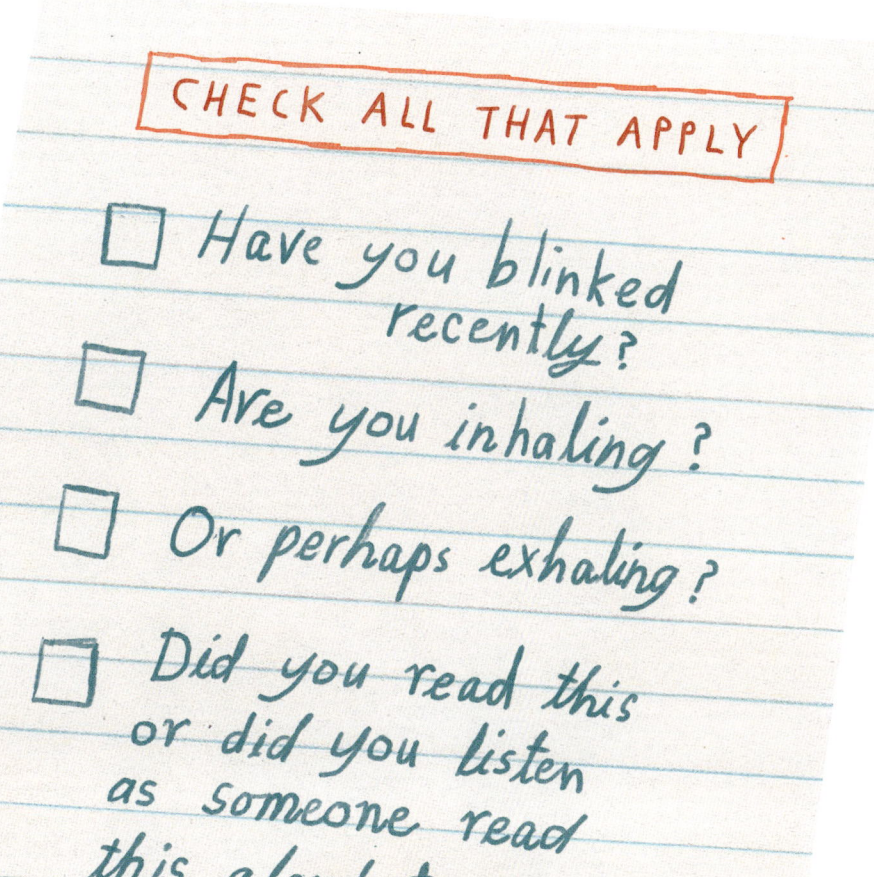

CHECK ALL THAT APPLY

☐ Have you blinked recently?
☐ Are you inhaling?
☐ Or perhaps exhaling?
☐ Did you read this or did you listen as someone read this aloud to you?

DID YOU CHECK ONE OR MORE OF THE ABOVE? OKAY, GOOD, YOU ARE ALIVE. YOU ARE READY TO GO.

DRAWING IS... TRAVELING

HERE'S A BLANK PAGE.

YOU CAN DRAW ANYTHING! BUT, NO IDEA IS COMING.

BECAUSE... TOO MUCH BLANKNESS.

WELL, YOU JUST NEED TWO THINGS.

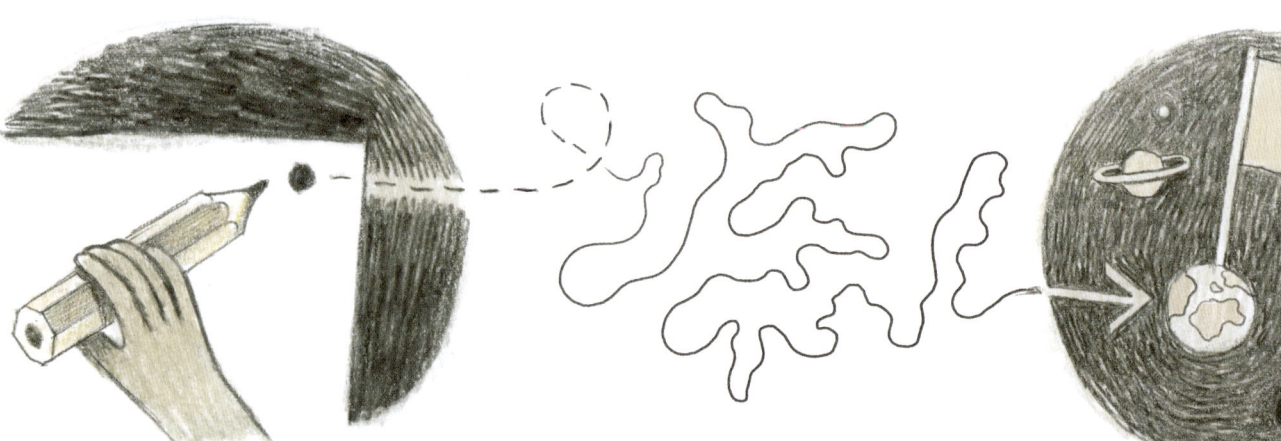

THE DOT IS LIKE A POINT ON A MAP. THE LINE TAKES YOU... SOMEWHERE.

TRY LINES *with different qualities*

WHAT HAPPENS WHEN YOU COMBINE DOTS AND LINES WITH DIFFERENT QUALITIES?

DOTS WITHIN CIRCLES... ARE THESE EYES? OR WHEELS?

TRY PLACING LINES CLOSE TOGETHER.  DOES IT SUGGEST MOTION?

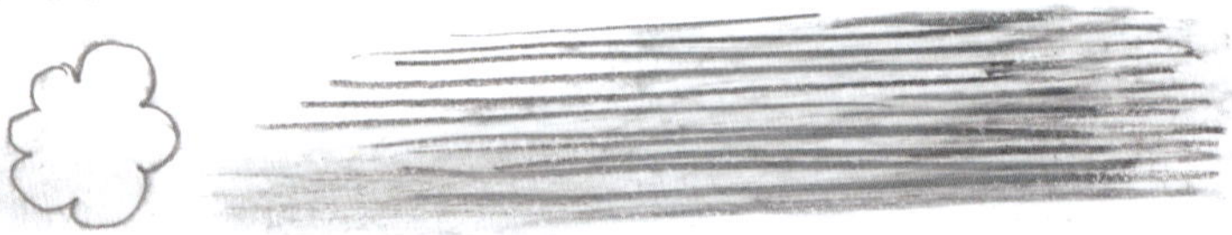

LAYER WHITE OR LIGHT-GRAY COLORED PENCIL OVER THE TOP.

← NOW IT ALMOST LOOKS LIKE PAINT.

TO CREATE A SENSE OF GLOWING, "DRAW" INTO SCRIBBLED TONE WITH AN ERASER. →

IF FAST IS NOT YOUR THING, THERE ARE SLOW WAYS TO GET PLACES... SUCH AS HITCHHIKING ON THE BACK OF A VERY SLOW CREATURE.

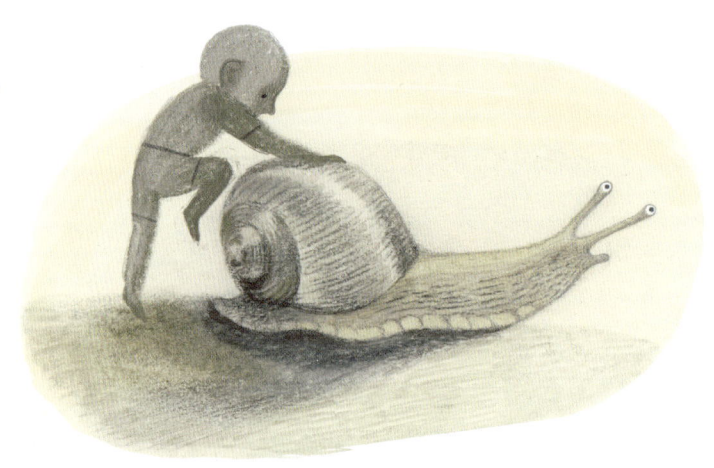

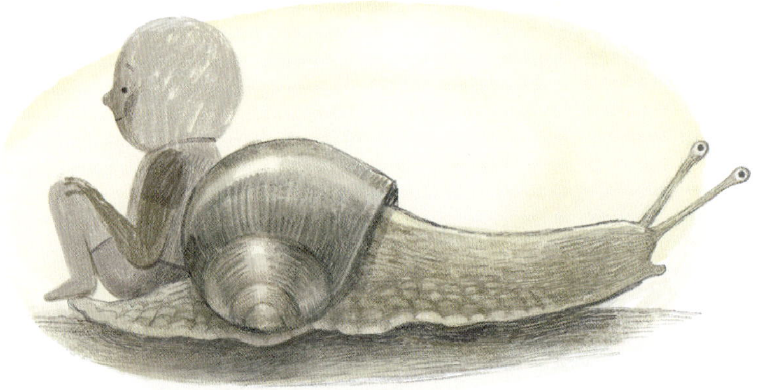

TRY SCALE

comparative size

LET'S TRY SHIFTING THE SENSE OF SCALE IN THIS SCENE:

 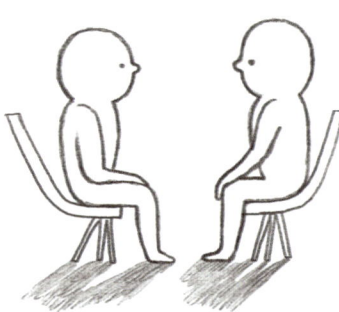 

← HERE'S YOU AND ME.

LET'S ADD SHADOWS SO IT FEELS REAL.

WE'RE HAVING TEA.

...ON JUPITER, GOSH! WE'RE QUITE TINY COMPARED TO THIS PLANET.

OR, WHAT IF THIS TEACUP WERE AS BIG AS A PLANET?

WE'D NEED A SAILBOAT TO GET ACROSS!

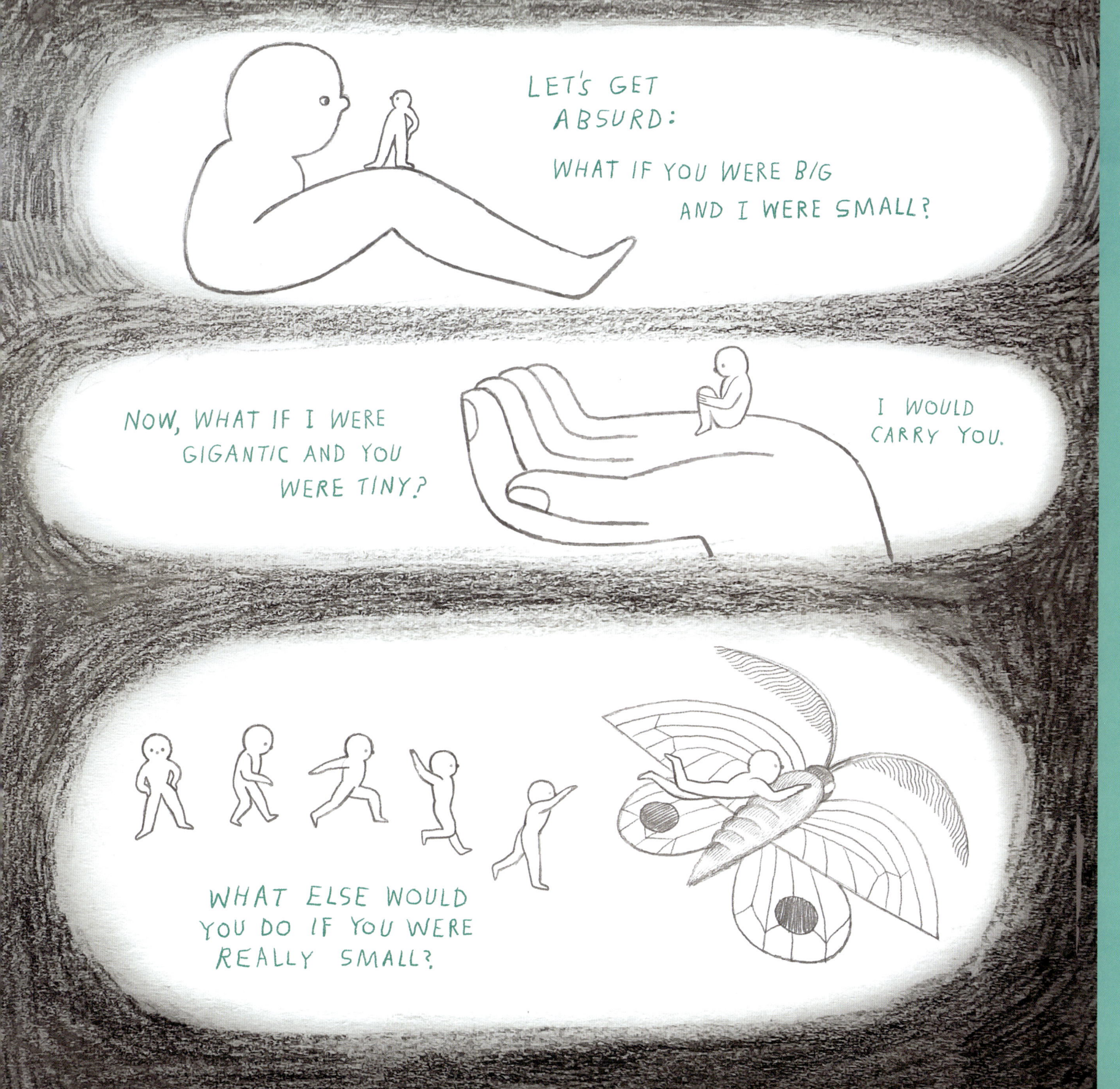

DRAWING IS... WONDERING

FAST OR SLOW, UP OR DOWN, AN IDEA FORMS, BUT THERE ARE MORE QUESTIONS STILL.

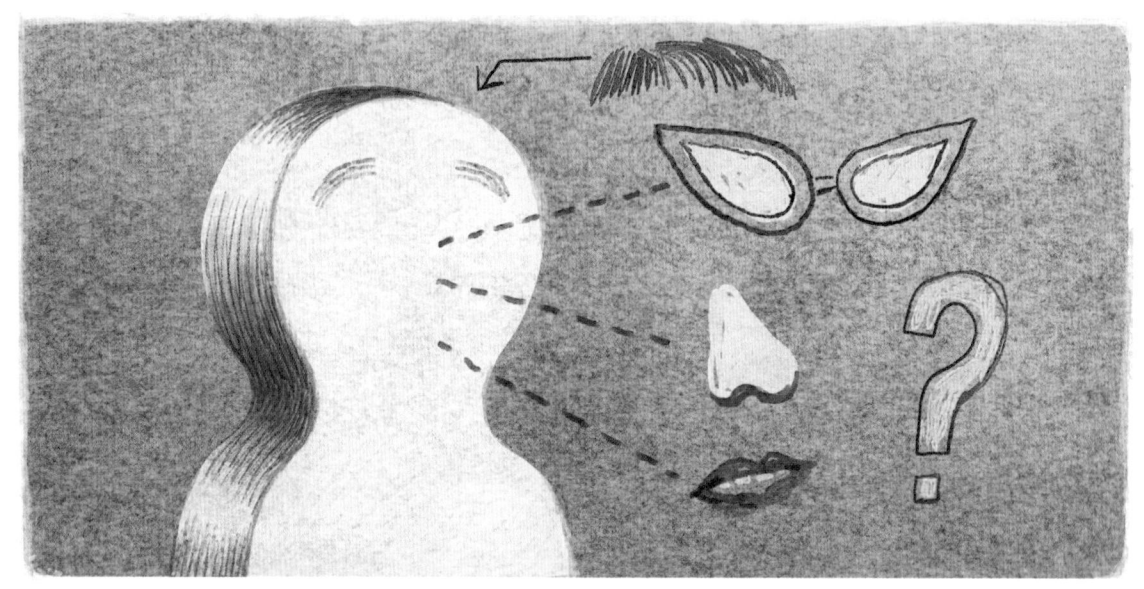

DO I DRAW MYSELF? IT NEVER ENDS UP LOOKING LIKE ME.

I KNOW, I'LL PUT ON AN ANIMAL HEAD.   FUN! LET'S TRY THE SAME WITH YOU.

HA HAAA, LOOK!   WE ARE TALKING IN DIFFERENT ANIMAL LANGUAGES.   IT'S CONFUSING!

WHAT MIGHT WE BE SAYING TO EACH OTHER?

CAN YOU IMAGINE WHAT WE ARE THINKING AND NOT SAYING?

TRYING TO GUESS WHAT OTHERS ARE THINKING IS WHAT MAKES PEOPLE-WATCHING SO INTERESTING.

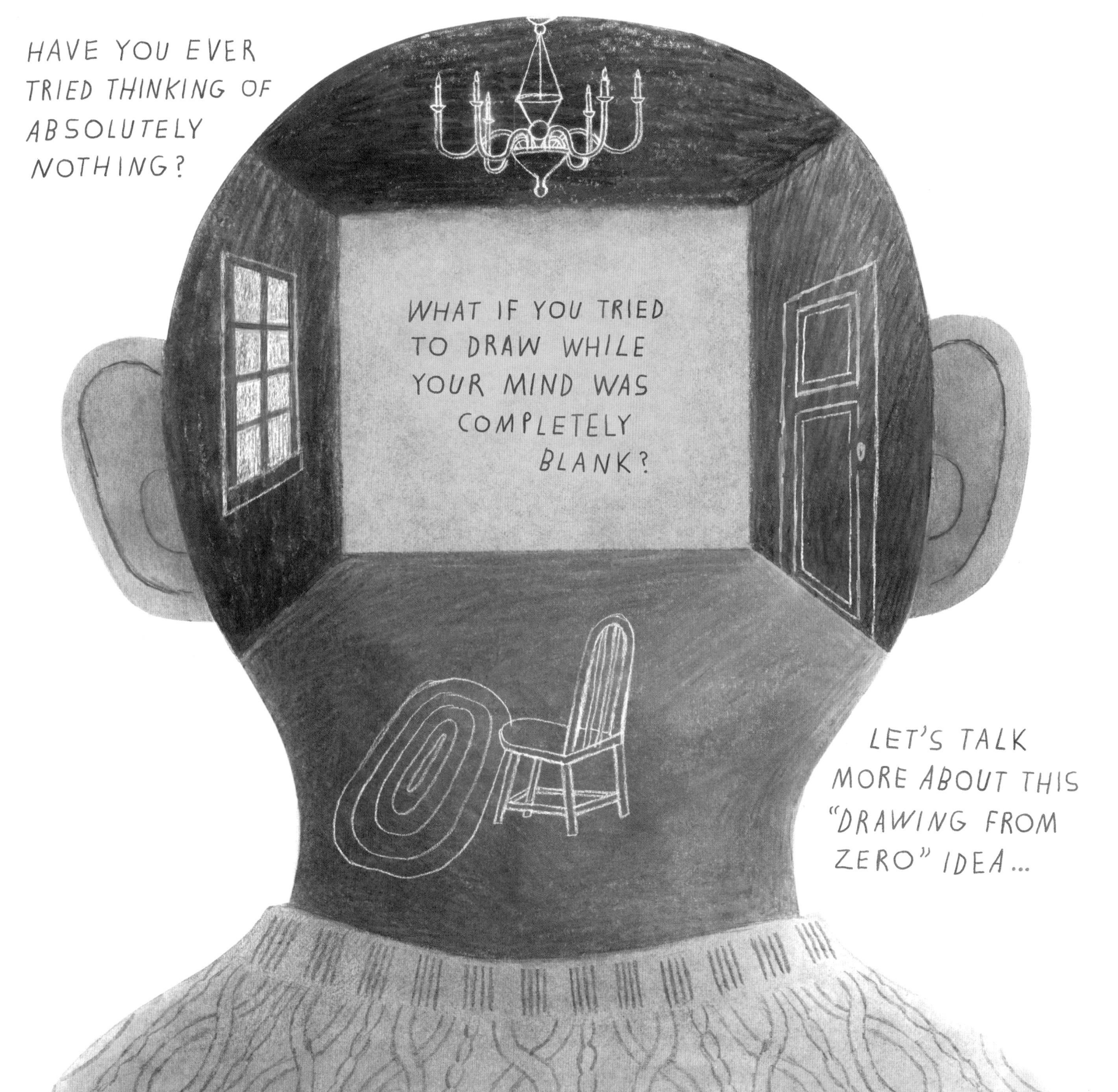

STARTING WITH ZERO FORETHOUGHT WAS A FAVORITE METHOD OF THE SURREALISTS— WRITERS AND ARTISTS WHO BEGAN A MOVEMENT IN 1924.

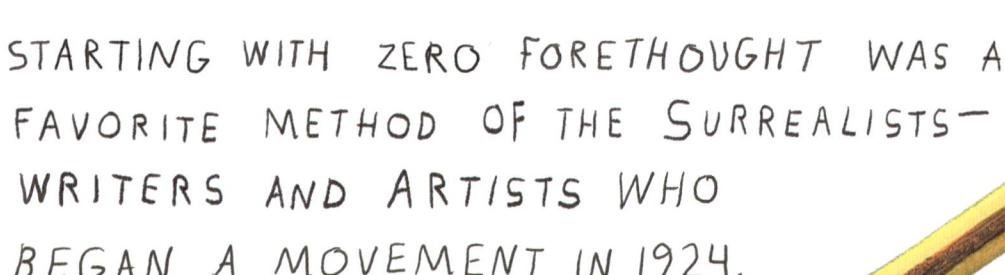
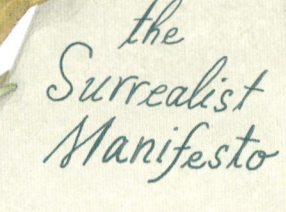

the Surrealist Manifesto

LED BY THE POET ANDRÉ BRETON, THEY INVENTED DRAWING AND WRITING GAMES IN WHICH THEY SPONTANEOUSLY SCRIBBLED, DREW OVER THE TOP OF EACH OTHER'S DRAWINGS AND ALLOWED FOR *"the intervention of the irrational,"* WHICH I TAKE TO MEAN "THE COURAGE TO BE SERIOUSLY SILLY."

Try a surrealist game called Exquisite Corpse. (YOU NEED THREE PEOPLE)

Fold a paper into thirds. The first person draws a head on the upper section.

Make sure the lines for the neck cross onto the middle section.

SO, ON THE PAGE, YOU MAKE IT UP AS YOU GO.

YOU ARE A KIND OF INVENTOR, SURPRISING EVEN YOURSELF AT TIMES.

YOU'RE SURPRISED BECAUSE YOU DIDN'T KNOW HOW IT WOULD TURN OUT.

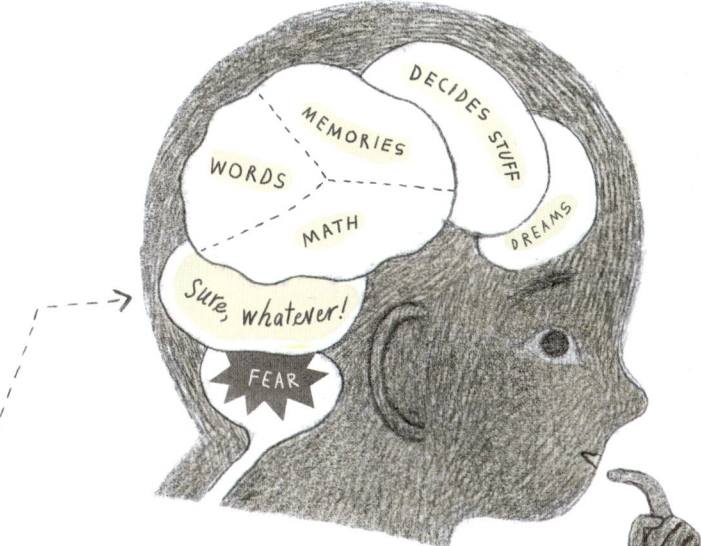

CAN YOU FIND AT LEAST A CORNER OF YOUR BRAIN THAT IS COMFORTABLE WITH NOT-KNOWING?

Then fold the drawing under, so the next person can't see the details.

The second person draws the neck and torso, with lines for the legs crossing the final fold.

The final person draws the rest of the legs and adds feet or shoes.

DRAWING IS... FOCUSING

HOW DOES YOUR SKETCHBOOK REVEAL WHAT YOU ARE PAYING ATTENTION TO?

LET'S ZOOM IN. WHAT ELSE IS THERE?

LOOK CLOSER.

TRY CONTRAST

create a focal point by placing dark and light tones together

HERE'S A SCENE WITH SOME STRANGE WEATHER.

PLANTS ARE GROWING, CREATURES ARE HIDING.

IT'S GETTING CROWDED NOW.

BUT I'M REALLY INTERESTED IN THIS OWL HUDDLED AGAINST THE TREE.

LET'S PUT THE DARKEST AND BRIGHTEST TONES AROUND IT.

MAYBE THE OWL SITS IN A DARK HOLE?

DRAWING IS... FEELING

LET'S DIP BELOW THE SURFACE NOW. HOW CAN DRAWING HINT AT WHAT'S INSIDE?

WHAT EMOTIONS DO THESE FACES EXPRESS?
THE EYEBROWS SAY A LOT.

HERE'S AN EXERCISE I'VE TRIED:
FILL A PAGE WITH CIRCLES. ADD NOSES, EYES, MOUTHS.
ADJUST THE EYEBROW POSITIONS SLIGHTLY TO CREATE
DIFFERENT EXPRESSIONS.

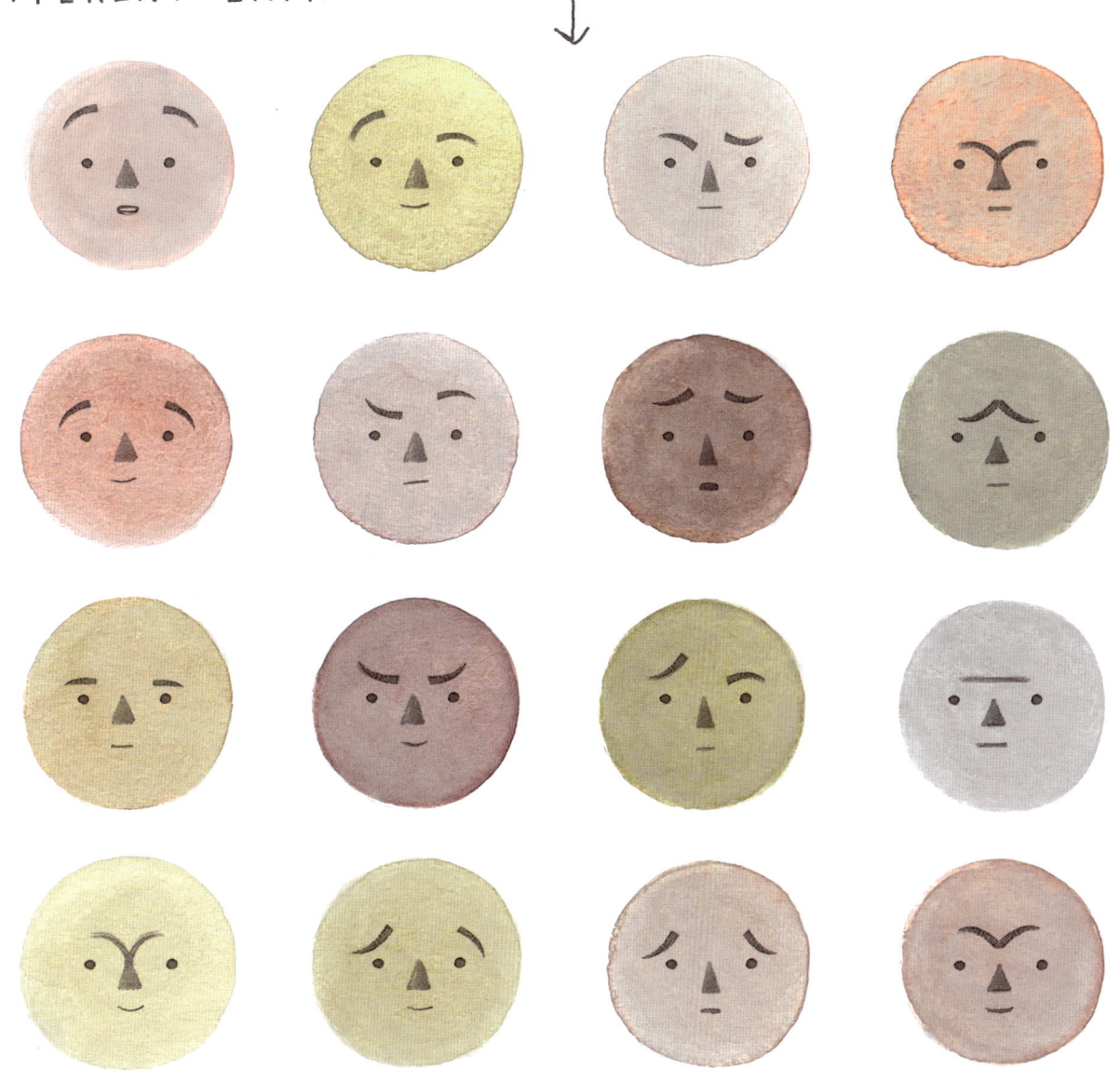

(I borrowed this from Ivan Brunetti, who said he got it from Chris Ware—both are genius-level comics artists.)

CHECK IN WITH YOURSELF.

HOW ARE YOU FEELING TODAY?

HOW WOULD YOU RATHER FEEL?

SOMETIMES I DRAW THESE INNER-SELF PORTRAITS AS A WAY OF TRACKING MY MOOD.

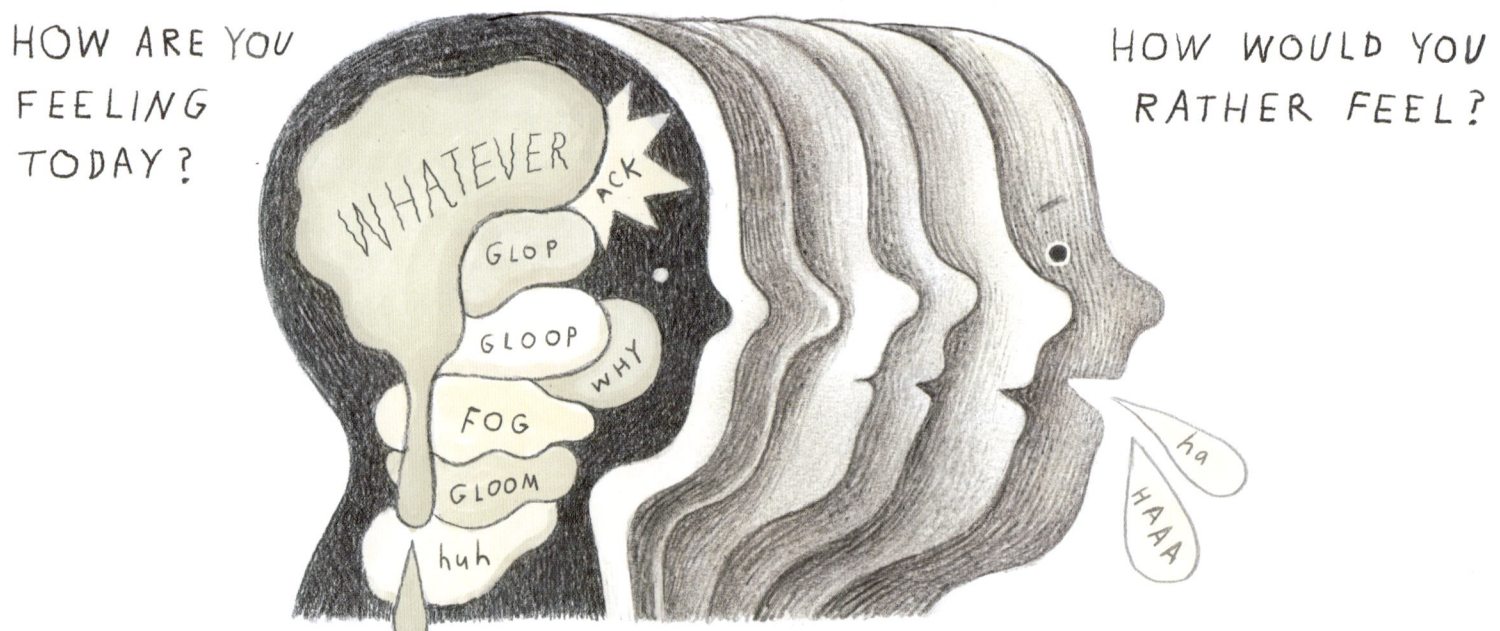

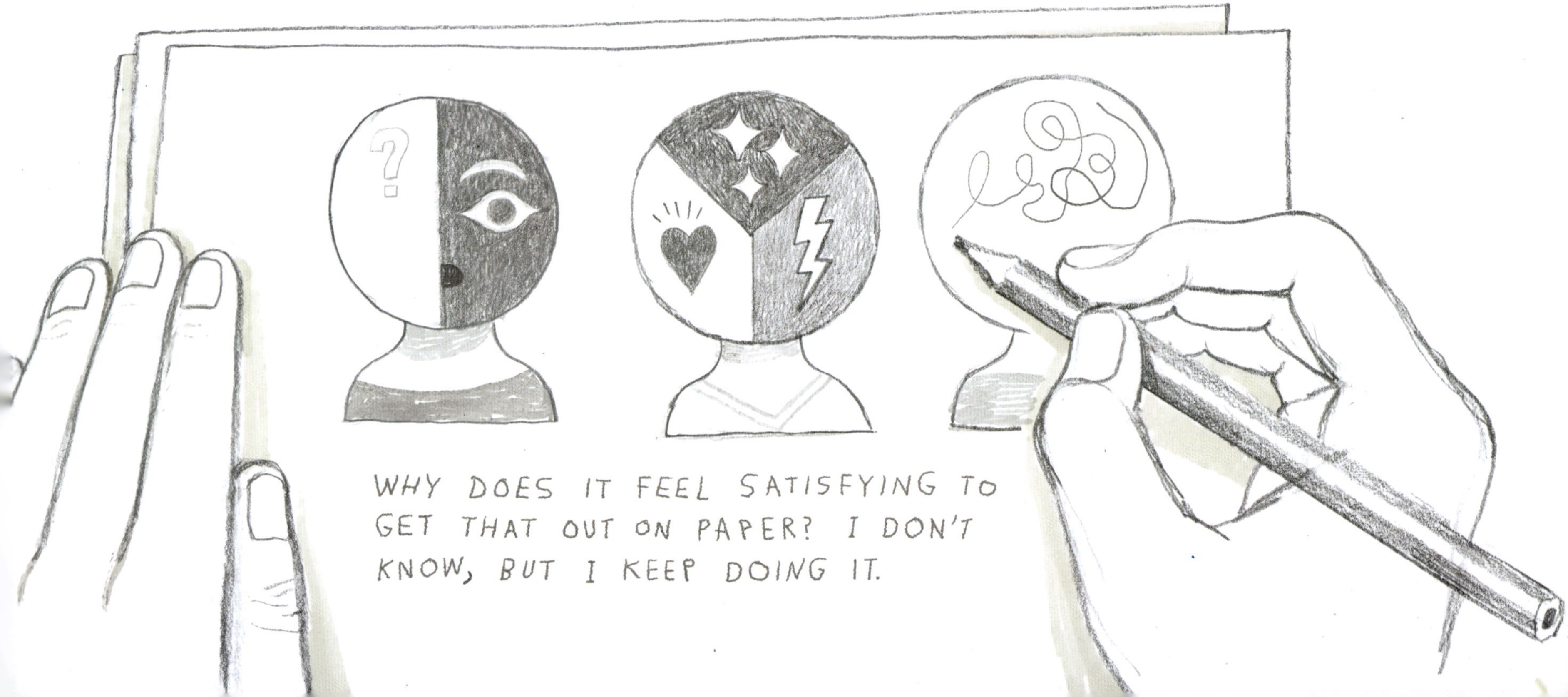

YOU CAN PUT FEELING INTO THE LINE ITSELF. CY TWOMBLY, AN ARTIST WHO CREATED SPECTACULARLY LARGE SCRIBBLE-PAINTINGS, SAID,

"The line is the FEELING, from a soft thing, a dreamy thing, to something HARD, something ARID, something LONELY, something ENDING, something BEGINNING."

HE USED TO DRAW IN BED AFTER DARK IN ORDER TO FOCUS ON THE PURE EXPERIENCE OF MAKING LINES.

LIGHTS OUT, SHALL WE TRY? HOW DOES THE LINE FEEL WHEN YOU DRAW IN THE DARK? Hey... are you still awake?

★INTER-

Bravo! You have reached the middle of this book! You deserve a break. A randomness-filled moment of pause.

I'm going to suggest you put on some loud music and gaze at these cute baby donkeys for five minutes.

Pausing a project to gaze at something completely different will open your mind to new solutions. Stopping is part of the creative process!

Follow these steps to draw your own baby donkey.

-MISSION ★

Why baby donkeys?

According to a study from Hiroshima University, there is a scientific basis for the human urge to gaze at cute things.

Study participants stared at photos of adorable puppies before attempting complex tasks. It improved their concentration and decreased stress levels.

Flip to this page whenever you need a reset!

★ ★ ★

1. 2. 3. 4. 5.

start with shapes and add legs →

DRAWING IS... GROWING

IT'S HARD TO RECOGNIZE PROGRESS. KEEP A SKETCHBOOK, TRACK YOUR GROWTH OVER TIME. WHEN YOU FLIP BACK TO A DRAWING FROM A YEAR AGO, YOU'LL BE SURPRISED AT HOW FAR YOU'VE COME.

↑ HERE'S A DRAWING I MADE AS A KID, AT AGE FOUR.

(Bugs, I think?)

LATER, AGE SIX, A FOUR-ARMED FIGURE.
(Was I an early Surrealist?)

↰ HERE'S A BUTTERFLY, FROM AGE SEVEN.

↰ AND 39 YEARS LATER, ANOTHER BUTTERFLY.

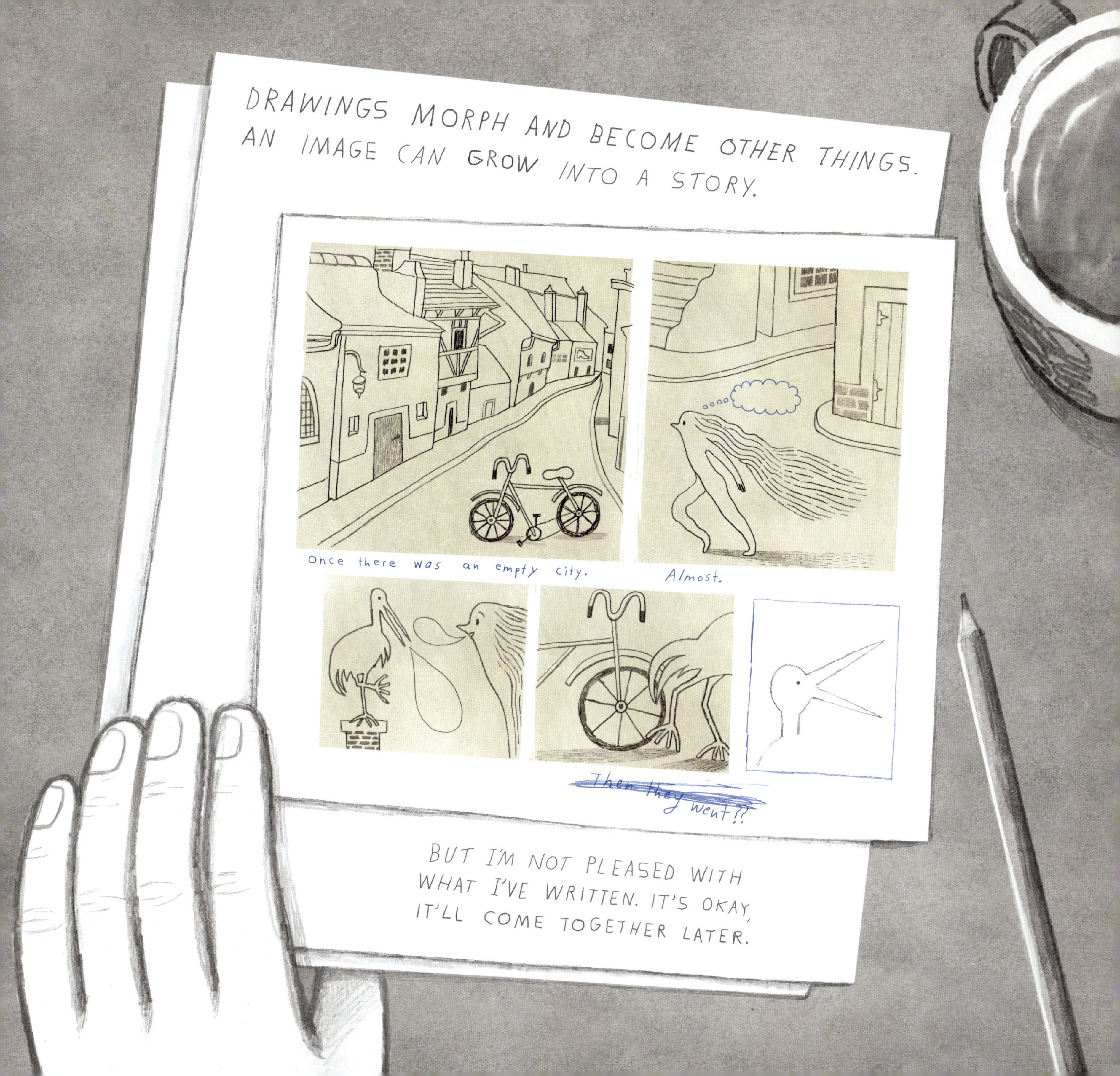
DRAWINGS MORPH AND BECOME OTHER THINGS. AN IMAGE CAN GROW INTO A STORY.
Once there was an empty city.
Almost.
~~Then they~~ went??
BUT I'M NOT PLEASED WITH WHAT I'VE WRITTEN. IT'S OKAY, IT'LL COME TOGETHER LATER.

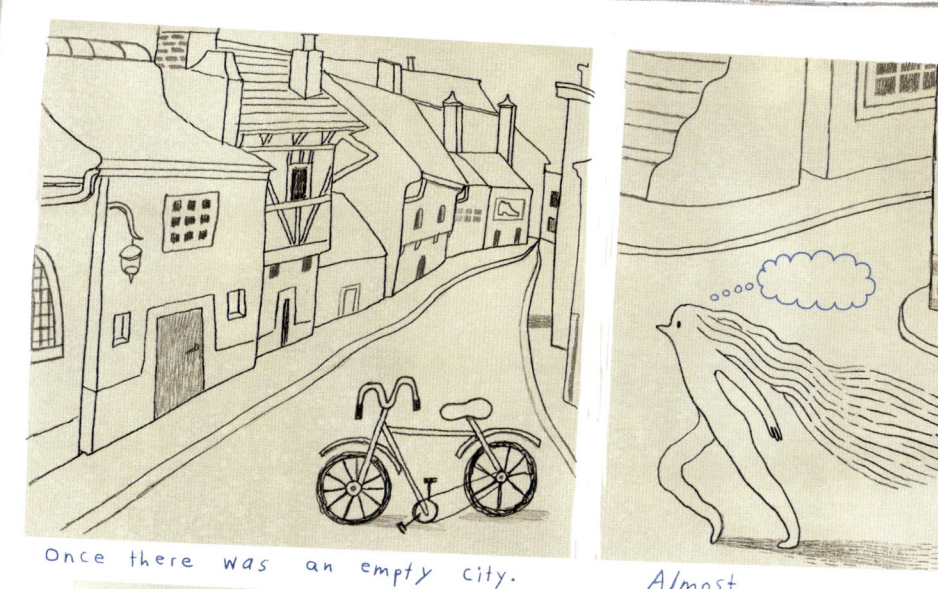

TRY DRAWING SOMETHING REALLY HARD, JUST BECAUSE IT'S HARD. WHEN LOOKING FOR A CHALLENGE, YOU SEE DIFFERENTLY.

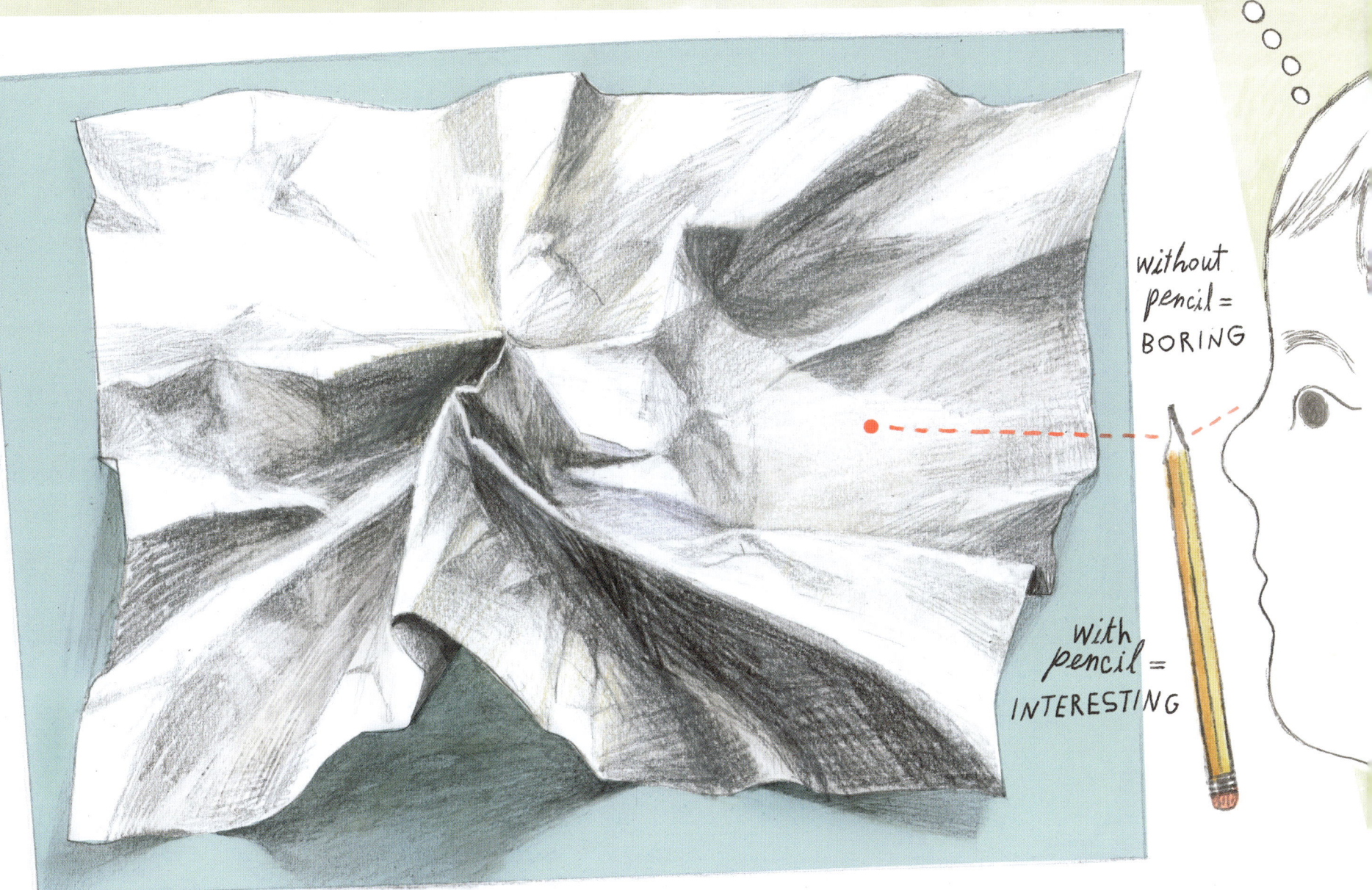

without pencil = BORING

with pencil = INTERESTING

EVEN A CRUMPLED PIECE OF PAPER CAN BECOME *FASCINATING.*

TRY TEXTURE

use lines to create different surface illusions

TEXTURE GIVES THE ILLUSION THAT A THING WOULD FEEL A CERTAIN WAY IF YOU REACHED INSIDE THE DRAWING TO TOUCH IT.

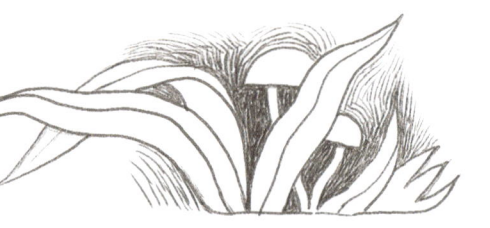

LOOK CLOSELY...

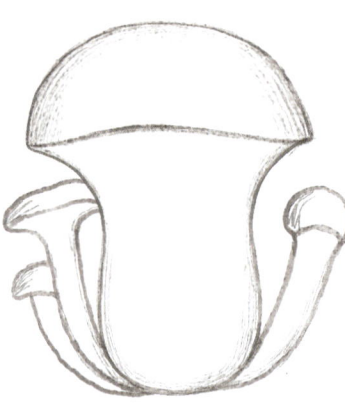

DO YOU THINK THIS MUSHROOM FEELS SMOOTH?

THIS ONE IS FURRY.

THIS MUSHROOM IS SLIMY.

THIS ONE IS HARD, LIKE TREE BARK. (IT'S CALLED "TURKEY TAIL" FOR OBVIOUS REASONS.)

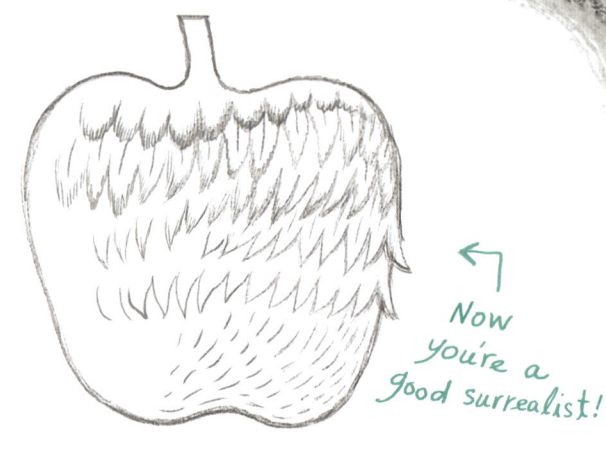

WHAT IF YOU PUT A TEXTURE WHERE IT DOESN'T BELONG?

Now you're a good surrealist!

TUTORIAL #4

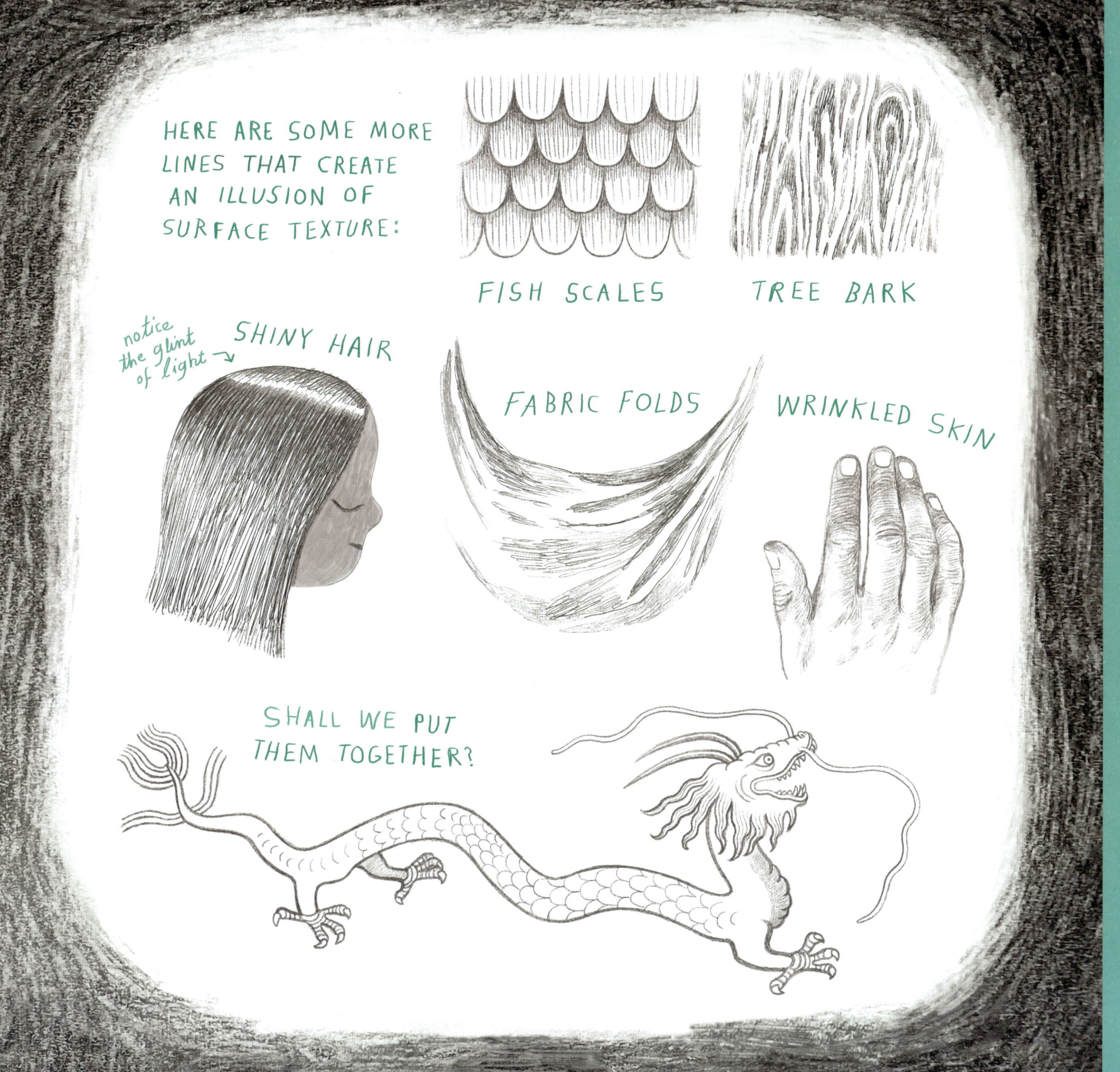

HERE ARE SOME MORE LINES THAT CREATE AN ILLUSION OF SURFACE TEXTURE:

FISH SCALES

TREE BARK

notice the glint of light → SHINY HAIR

FABRIC FOLDS

WRINKLED SKIN

SHALL WE PUT THEM TOGETHER?

DRAWING IS... NOT-KNOWING

WHEN YOU BEGIN A DRAWING, YOU DON'T KNOW IF YOU'LL LIKE THE RESULT.

Signs: ROAD NOT IMPROVED · ROUND-A-BOUT OF INDECISION · ENDLESS CONSTRUCTION · DETOUR

PERHAPS THE WORD "DRAWING" — THE <u>NOUN</u>, THE <u>RESULT</u> — IS PART OF THE PROBLEM. IT CAN BE LOADED WITH EXPECTATION. DO YOU EVER THINK LIKE THIS?

I'm going to make a drawing...

and then I can:

A. FRAME IT
B. SELL IT
C. HANG IT IN A MUSEUM

(frame labeled AMAZINGNESS)

OR AT LEAST THIS DRAWING WILL TRANSLATE MY IDEA FROM <u>BRAIN</u> TO <u>HAND</u> TO <u>PAPER</u> — right?

TA-DA

HOWEVER, THIS IS NOT ALWAYS THE CASE.
WHAT IF WE CALL THE "DRAWING" BY ANOTHER NAME? SOMETHING WITH FEWER ASSUMPTIONS? TRY THESE:

1. LOOK AT THIS ~~drawing~~ EXPERIMENT.

2. I WANT TO SHOW YOU MY ~~drawing~~ DRAFT.

3. CHECK OUT MY SKETCHBOOK, I'VE MADE A NEW ~~drawing~~ FATHOGRAM.*

*an oceanography term for a chart that maps the depths

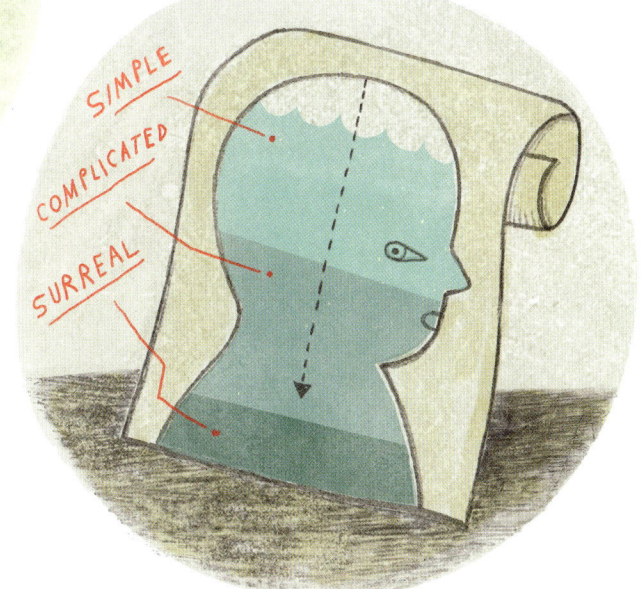

JEAN-MICHEL BASQUIAT WAS AN AMERICAN ARTIST WHO MIXED IMAGES WITH WORDS ON CANVAS. HE SAID,

"I don't think about art while I'm working. I try to think about LIFE."

PART OF NOT-KNOWING IS WONDERING HOW YOU'LL FIND TIME TO DRAW. YOU'RE BUSY, LOTS TO DO.

DRAW YOUR IDEAL STUNT DOUBLE.

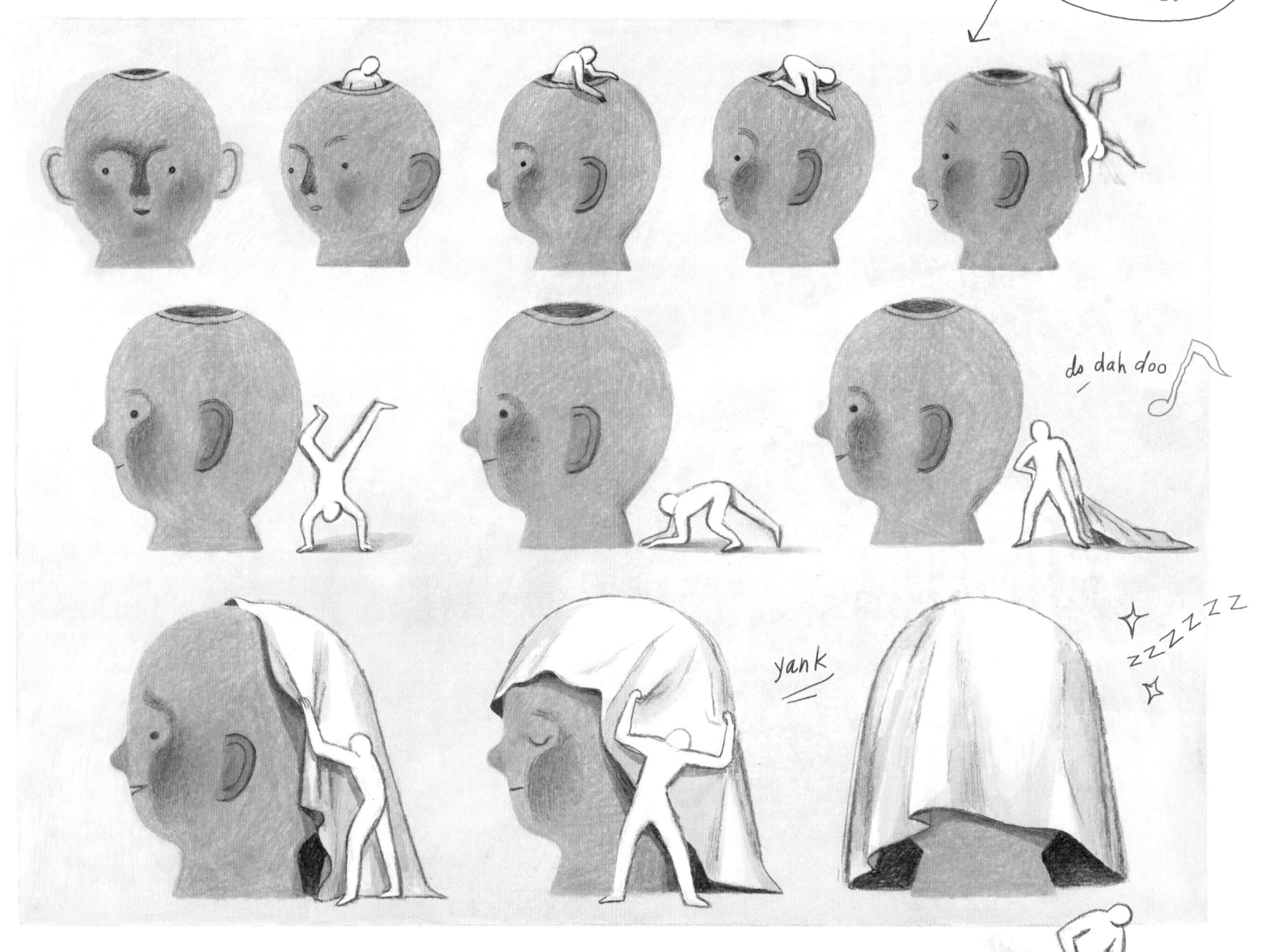

CAN YOUR STUNT DOUBLE TAKE OVER SO YOU CAN DOODLE, DAYDREAM, EVEN GET A LITTLE BORED?

BRING A SKETCHPAD ALONG ON YOUR NEXT CAR, BUS OR TRAIN RIDE.

YOU MAY NOT LOVE THE WOBBLY RESULTS, BUT YOU WILL HAVE FOUND MORE TIME TO DRAW.

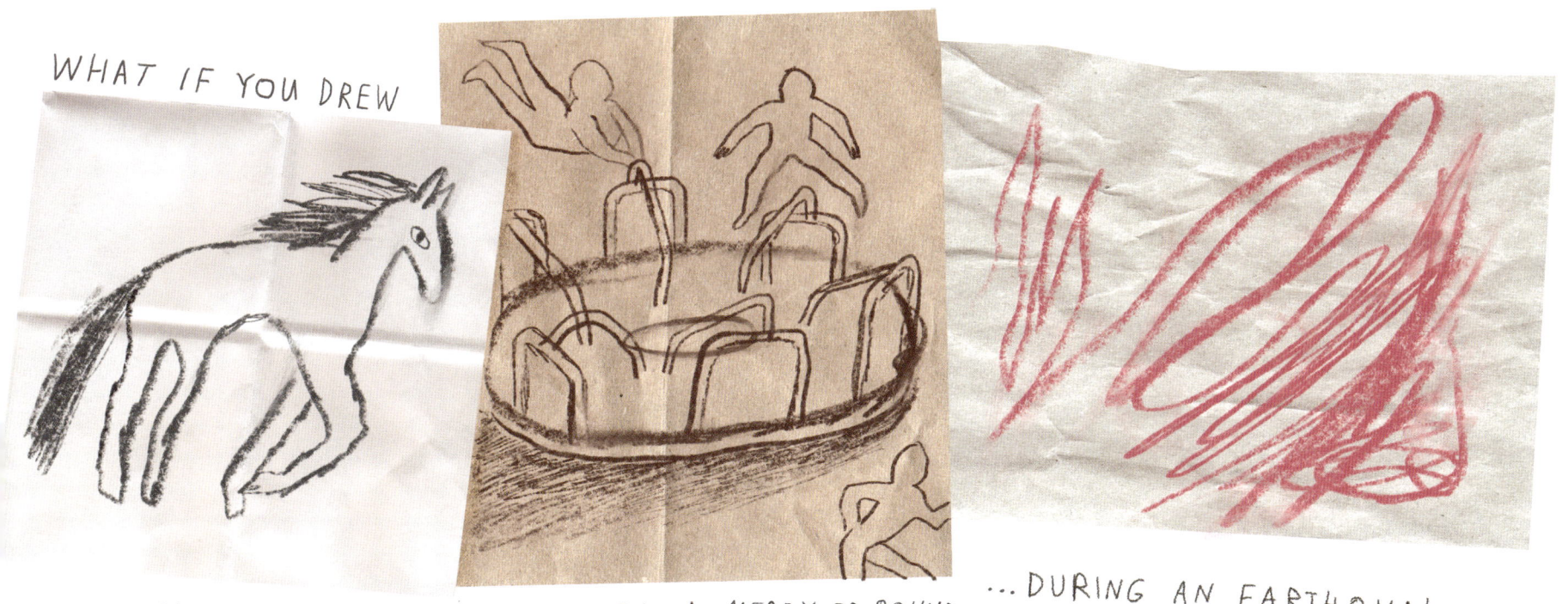

WHAT IF YOU DREW

...ON HORSEBACK?

...ON A MERRY-GO-ROUND?

...DURING AN EARTHQUAKE? (Joking! I would never recommend that.)

WHILE YOU ARE HOPING FOR BIG IDEAS TO ARRIVE...

TRY REPETITIVE DOODLING, A PATTERN MADE OF LINES OR SHAPES. MOMENTUM IS KEY HERE. JUST KEEP YOUR HAND IN MOTION.

WHAT GIVES YOU A SMALL BURST OF SATISFACTION? LOOPS, WAVES, DOTS?

CAN YOU TRANSFORM ANXIETY BY DOODLING A PATTERN UNTIL YOU FEEL CALM?

YAYOI KUSAMA BECAME FAMOUS FOR HER LIFELONG FIXATION

WITH POLKA DOTS— COVERING PAINTINGS, GIANT PUMPKINS, ENTIRE ROOMS,

LIVE HORSES, EVEN **HERSELF**, WITH DOTS!

SHE HAS SPOKEN PUBLICLY ABOUT HER STRUGGLE WITH DEPRESSION AND SEEKING REFUGE IN HER ART PRACTICE.

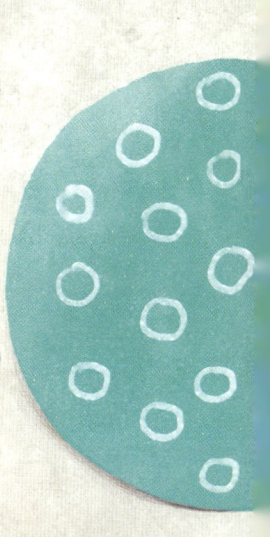

YAYOI SAID, "Polka dots can't stay alone... two or three polka dots become movement.

Polka dots are a way to infinity."

P O W !!

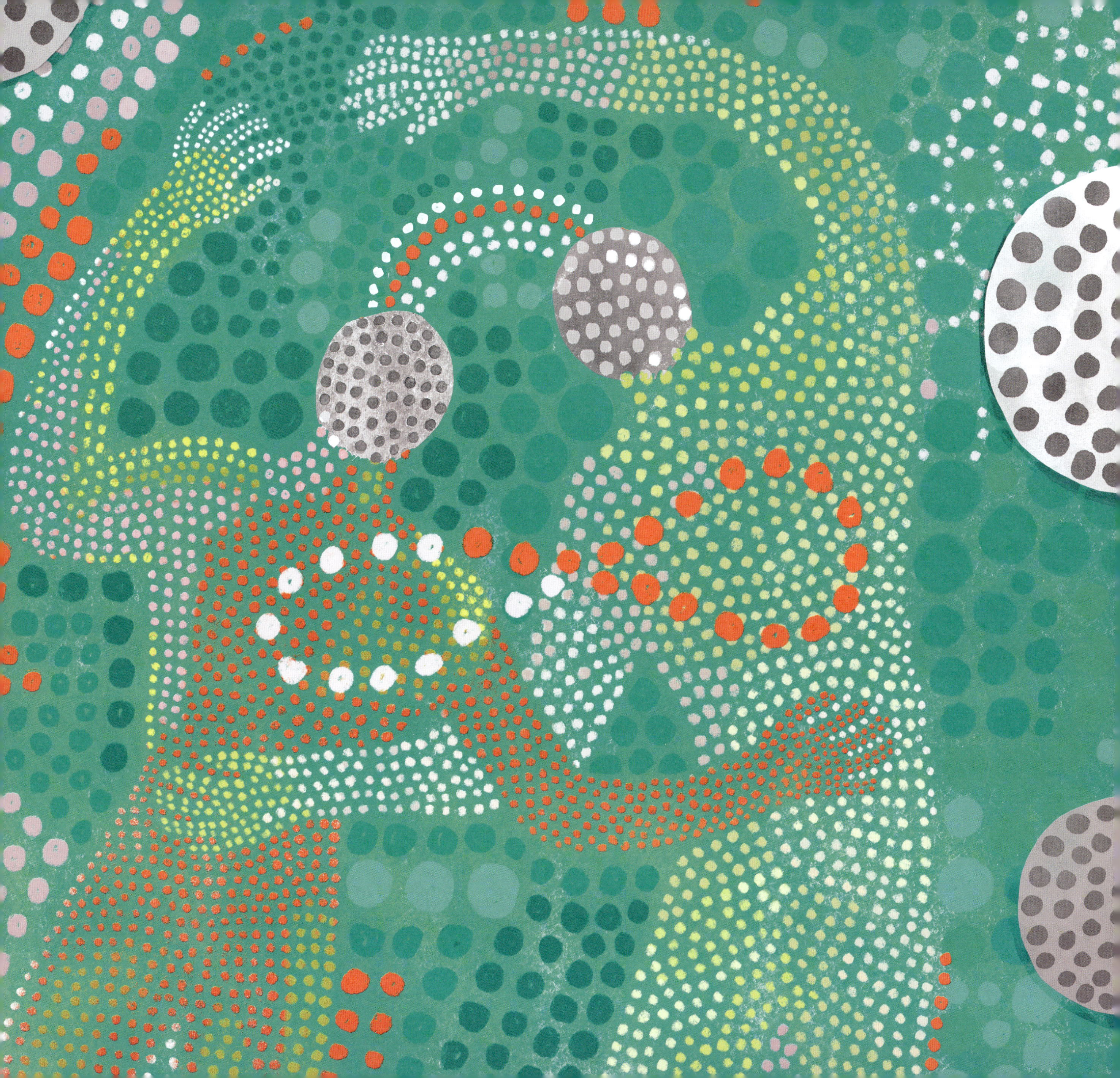

TRY PATTERN

a repeating combination of marks, lines or shapes

HERE ARE SOME FAVORITE PATTERNS OF OTHER ARTISTS:

TRY A SLOW SPIRAL. BEGIN IN THE CENTER AND FILL THE PAGE.

← THIS IS EXPERIMENTAL COMICS EXPERT LYNDA BARRY'S ADVICE ABOUT HOW TO WARM UP.

Also, what else can a spiral be?

TUTORIAL #5

TRY PILING UP DOTS, LIKE YAYOI KUSAMA.

DRAW LOOPS AND FILL IN THE HOLES WITH COLOR, LIKE THE SCULPTOR ALEXANDER CALDER.

RUTH ASAWA, WHO WOVE METAL WIRES INTO GIANT DRIPPING BULBS, LIKED TO SKETCH WAVES AND LINK ENDLESS TRIANGLES ON THE PAGE.

OVER TIME, YOU'LL DISCOVER YOUR OWN FAVORITES.

HERE'S WHAT I LIKE: DRIPS

SCALLOPED SWOOPS LIKE WAVES ON A SHORE

TANGLES, LIKE COMPLICATED FUNGAL NETWORKS UNDERGROUND

DRAWING IS... MAGIC

YOU CAN MAKE TIME SLOW DOWN, STAND STILL.

YOU CAN DRAW YOUR WAY INTO A NEW MOOD.

YOU CAN EVEN DRAW YOUR OWN SENSE OF BELONGING.

QUEEN OF SOMEWHERE

INSIDE THE PAGES OF YOUR SKETCHBOOK, YOU ARE CREATING YOUR OWN, MAGICAL SOMEWHERE.

HERE ARE SOME PLACES THAT I'VE VISITED IN MY SKETCHBOOK:

magical library

tree house

remote island

I CAN FEEL SAFE, CALM, FAR AWAY.

Wait! WHAT ABOUT DRAWINGS THAT TURN OUT AWFUL? THOSE DON'T FEEL MAGICAL. HERE'S WHAT I THINK: IT'S NOBODY'S BUSINESS IF THE DRAWING IS GOOD OR BAD.

"so bad!"

What if it's not even your business?

NOT YOUR BIZ

YOUR BIZ

DECIDES STUFF

FEELINGS

SILLINESS CENTER

JUDGY PART

YOUR HAND AND YOUR IMAGINATION ARE WORKING TOGETHER. IT'S A MAGICAL PROCESS, REGARDLESS OF THE RESULT.

Watch out for the part of your brain that wants to QUIT!

LYNDA BARRY, WHO TEACHES A CLASS CALLED Writing the Unthinkable, ASKS:

"What if a bad drawing is what an IDEA looks like when it's being BORN?"

TRY ON THAT BELIEF. HOW DOES IT FEEL? IDEAS LANDING ON THE PAGE, YOUR HAND MAKING THE VISIBLE FROM THE INVISIBLE?

PRETTY MAGICAL.

AND ALL FROM THESE INGREDIENTS: A DOT AND A LINE.

THE DOT BECOMING A LINE IS A KIND OF GROWING. IT GOES SOMEWHERE.

CAN IT REACH THE FARTHEST EDGES OF YOUR MIND?

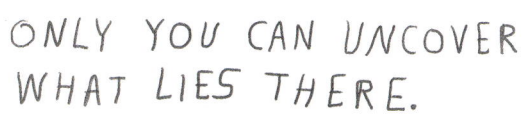

ONLY YOU CAN UNCOVER WHAT LIES THERE.

THE GOOD, THE BAD, THE UGLY, THE BIZARRE AND THE BEAUTIFUL.

YOU ARE THE DOCUMENTARIAN OF YOURSELF.

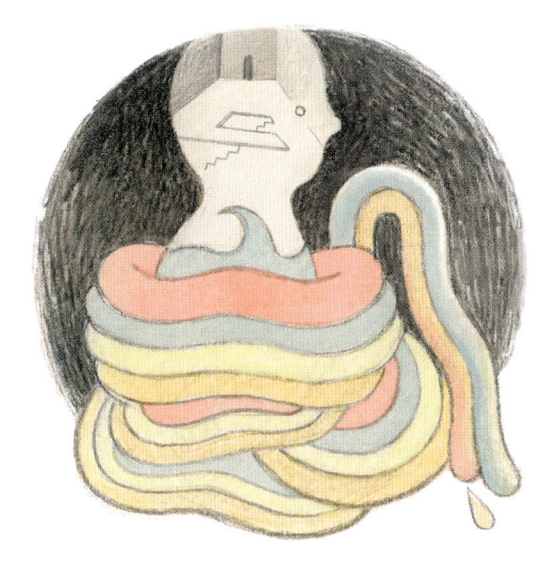

A DRAWING IS EVIDENCE... THAT YOU ARE ALIVE, YOU EXIST!
ALL YOU NEED IS SOMETHING TO DRAW ON.

SOMETHING TO DRAW WITH.

EMILY DICKINSON, AN AMERICAN POET, KEPT PAPER SCRAPS AND PENCILS IN ALL HER POCKETS, ALWAYS READY TO JOT DOWN AN IDEA.

hope is the thing with feathers

HERE'S WHAT SHE SAID ABOUT THE BLANK PAGE:

"NOTHING is the beginning of EVERYTHING."

WHERE IS ALL THIS HEADED, YOU WONDER?

ONE THING IS CERTAIN: WE'VE REACHED THE END OF THIS BOOK.

BUT YOU ARE JUST GETTING STARTED!

TRY THE EXERCISES IN THE PAGES AHEAD.
REPEAT THEM OVER TIME AND DISCOVER YOUR OWN
WORLD OF DOTS AND LINES, SHAPES AND PATTERNS.

BEFORE WE GO, SOME WIT AND WISDOM FROM OUR FRIEND HOKUSAI:

"From the age of six I had a mania for drawing the shapes of things.

When I was 50 I had published a universe of designs.

But all I have done before the age of 70 is not worth bothering with.

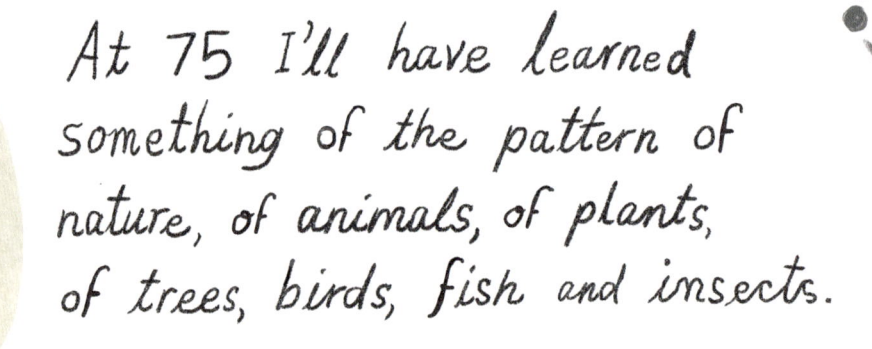

At 75 I'll have learned something of the pattern of nature, of animals, of plants, of trees, birds, fish and insects.

When I am 80 you will see real progress.
At 90 I shall have cut my way deeply into the mystery of life itself.
At 100, I shall be a marvelous artist.
At 110, everything I create; a dot, a line, will jump to life as never before."

EXERCISES

Launch your own practice — try this mini course of repeatable exercises...

1. OUTLINES AND SHAPES

See if you can spend most of the time looking at your subject, with only occasional glances to see where your pencil is touching the page. Try not picking up your pencil at all — the drawing can be made up of one really long line!

Tip:
Try using paper from the recycling bin for this exercise so that you feel less attached to the outcome.

RIVER ROCKS

Resist the urge to "label" things in your mind while you are drawing. What if you were simply observing shapes, angles, lines... and putting them on the page?

~~SLEEPING CAT~~ → FUZZY OVAL WITH POINTY TRIANGLES.

~~FACE WITH GLASSES~~ → ROUNDED SQUARE WITH LUMPY EDGE

DRAWING AS SEEING:

IN THESE REPEATABLE EXERCISES, THE AIM IS TO DRAW AS SLOWLY AS POSSIBLE.

CAN YOU SYNC YOUR HAND AND EYE MOVEMENTS SO THAT YOUR PENCIL GOES THE SPEED OF YOUR GAZE, WITHOUT RACING AHEAD?

(It's pretty hard!)

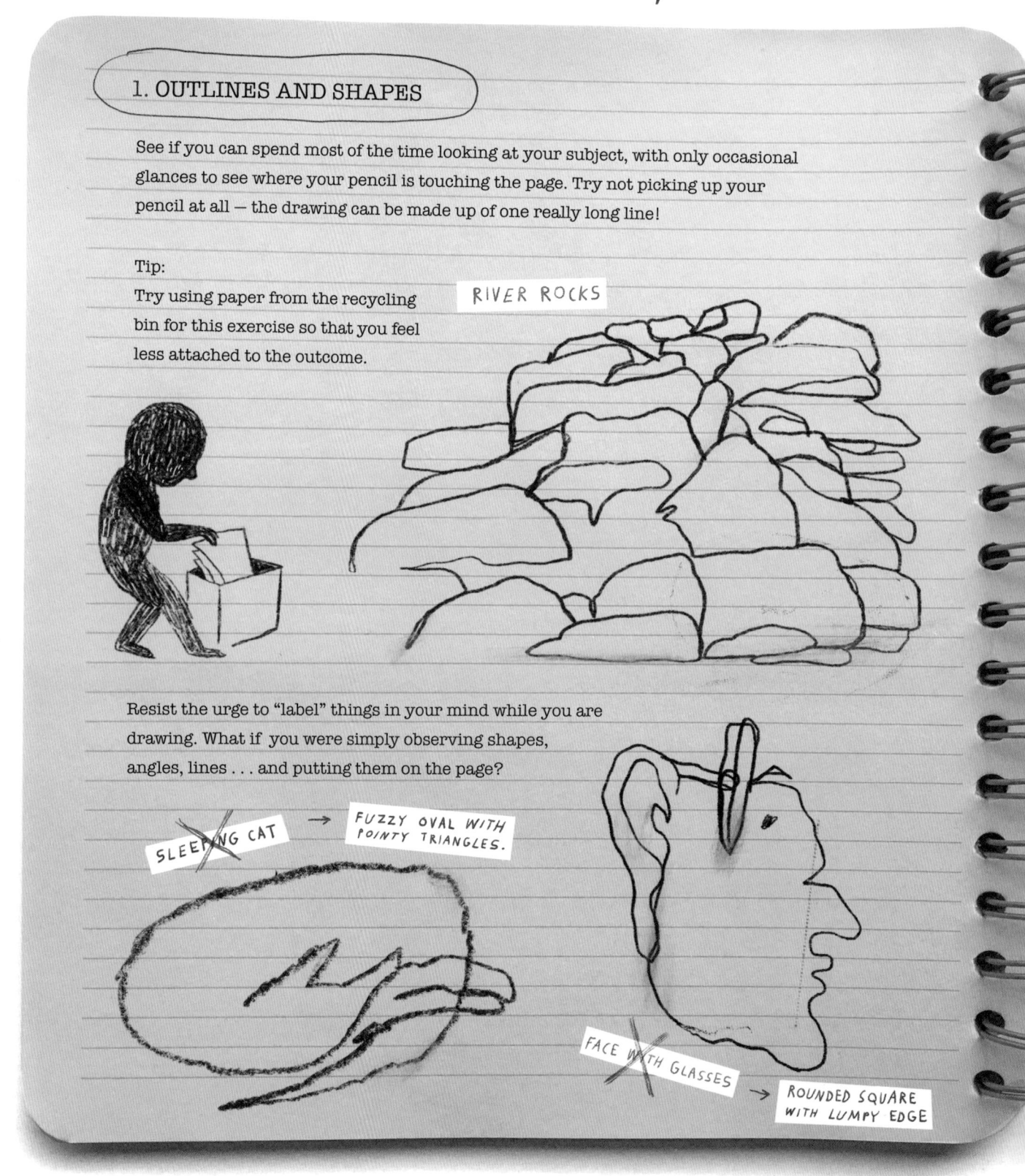

Take a small sketchbook with you everywhere. See how often you can dip in.

EXERCISES

2. NONDOMINANT HAND

Try using the hand you don't normally feel comfortable using. Start with a word or phrase. Write it large while standing over a sheet of paper on the ground and gripping the biggest paintbrush you have. Tape a paintbrush to a long stick and try that.

my left hand

This is a cat that I drew left-handed.

FLUFFY

Now try drawing something you see in front of you. Your nondominant hand moves slower, so it's even harder to keep your eye moving at the pace of your fingers. How slow can you go?
How many other ways can you make surprising lines?
Grip the pencil with your toes and try drawing with your foot.

TRY DRAWING AWKWARDLY:

SOME ARTISTS WRITE BACKWARDS IN ORDER TO PRACTICE SEEING THE LETTERS AS PURE SHAPES.

DO YOU KNOW WHAT THIS SAYS?

how about this?
(hold it up to a mirror)

EXERCISES

DRAW THE INVISIBLE:

CHECK IN WITH YOURSELF. HOW DOES YOUR INNER LANDSCAPE CHANGE OVER TIME?

✲

BE HONEST! REMEMBER TO POKE FUN AT YOURSELF SOMETIMES.

3. MIND PORTRAIT

Draw a circle. (Trace a jar lid if you like.) Add a neck and upper shoulders. Divide the circle into smaller pie slices. Add labels based on what's happening in the moment.

Labels in left portrait: DRINK 8 CUPS OF WATER, SUSPENSE, FUN PLANS, hope, WONDER, CONFUSION, ?, worry, OBLIGATIONS

Labels in right portrait: headache, JOY, AWE, SADNESS, !, REALIZATION

What's on your mind? Are different emotions occurring?
Is there one giant thing taking up most of your focus, or are you divided across many thoughts, ideas, concerns, to-do list items?

Put a bunch of portraits all on a large sheet of paper — a snapshot of condensed time!

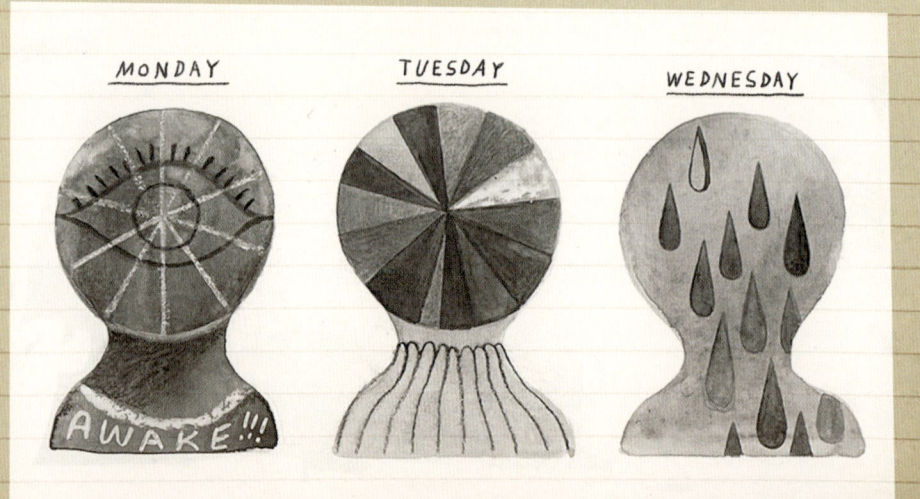

MONDAY — AWAKE!!! **TUESDAY** **WEDNESDAY**

4. MOOD PORTRAIT

What if the inside of your mind were a house? A room in a house? Or a wild, jungly place? Try making visual choices to evoke a mood. Maybe one color is dominant.

Is the lighting bright or shadowy? Is there rain, ice or sunshine pouring in through a window?

Is it crowded or empty?

Are there mysterious boxes stacked in the corner, like memories?

What about levels? You find different things in a cellar, attic or living room.

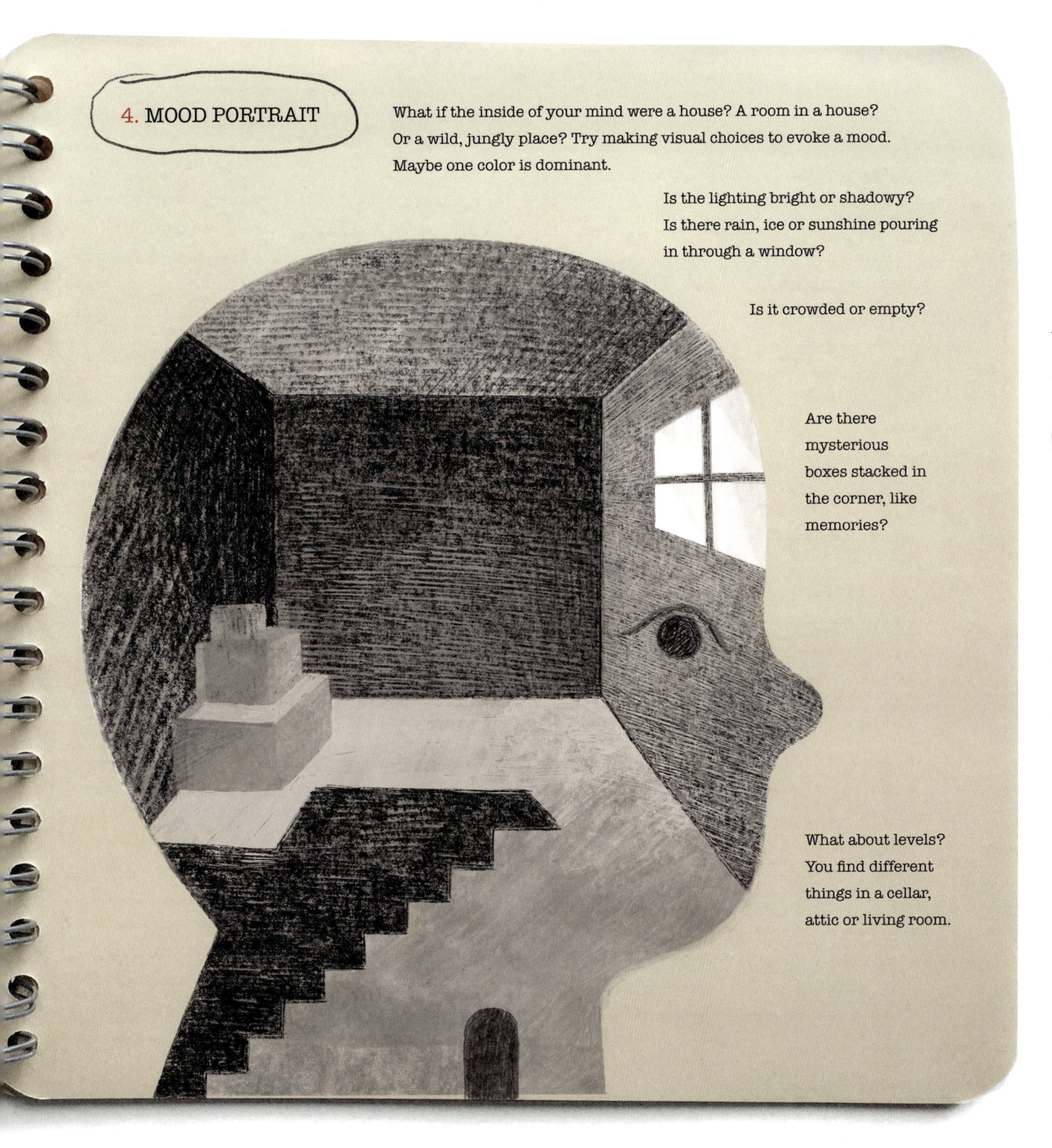

DO YOU HAVE TIME FOR A LOT OF DETAILS? THEN LOOK AT SOME PHOTOS FOR REFERENCE.

IN A RUSH, OR WANT TO AVOID DETAILS? DRAW BLOBS AND LABEL THEM.

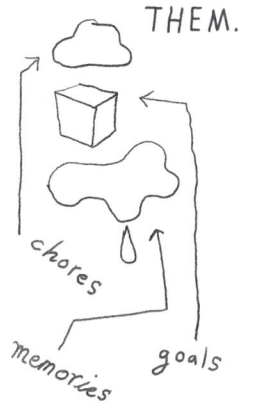

chores — memories — goals

EXERCISES

INTENTIONALLY BAD ART:

MAKE SOMETHING YOU'LL LIKELY HATE.

(You can always throw it in the recycling bin!)

WHAT IF YOU DON'T ENJOY THIS? TRY IT WITH A FRIEND! YOU CAN LAUGH AT EACH OTHER'S "TERRIBLE ART" AND NOT TAKE YOURSELVES SO SERIOUSLY.

5. FACE THE HARD STUFF

What are your artistic weak points? Drawing hands, feet, ears... bicycles, cars? Challenge yourself to draw whatever you find difficult every day for a week.

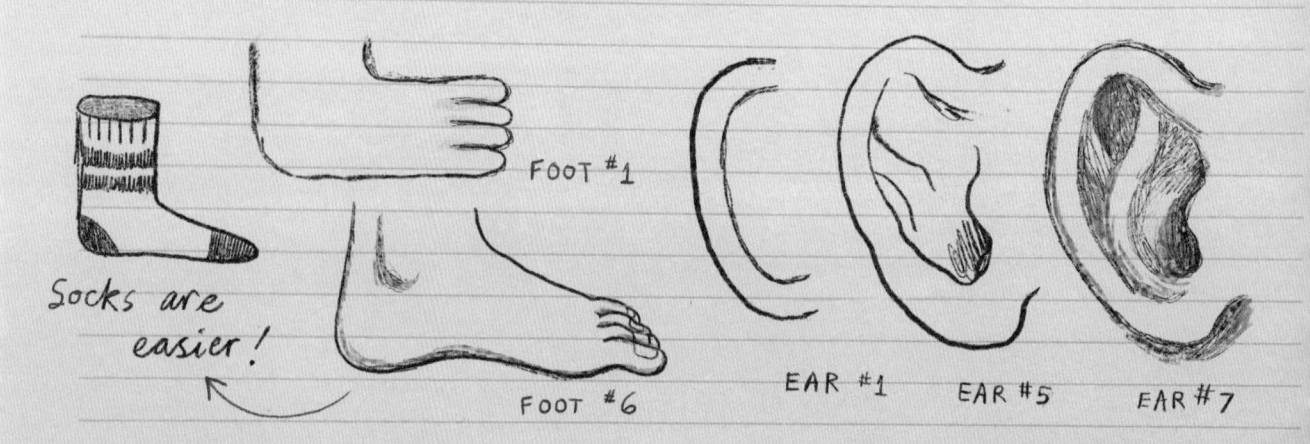

Socks are easier!

FOOT #1

FOOT #6

EAR #1   EAR #5   EAR #7

After this exercise, either you improve or you get creative about how to avoid drawing the hard thing in the future, which is also a choice you can make!

Drawing involves a constant series of choices. What you choose NOT to draw is just as important as what you decide TO draw.

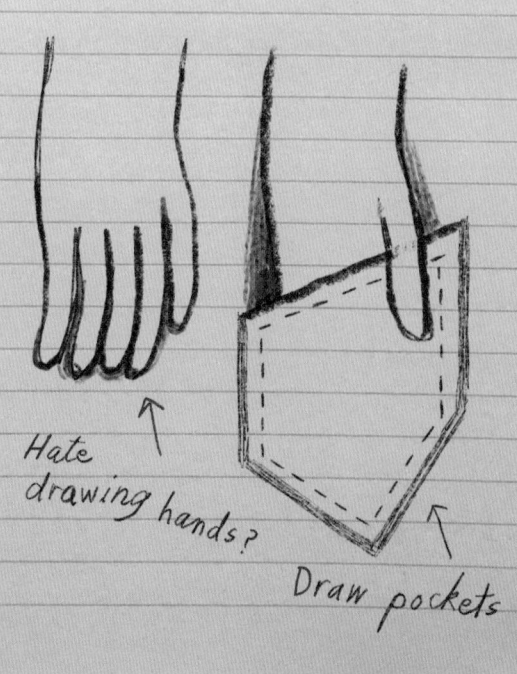

Hate drawing hands?

Draw pockets

6. MONTH-LONG STUDY

Get to know one subject really well! Avoid time wasted on indecision: any time you open your sketchbook that month, you'll already know what you're going to draw.

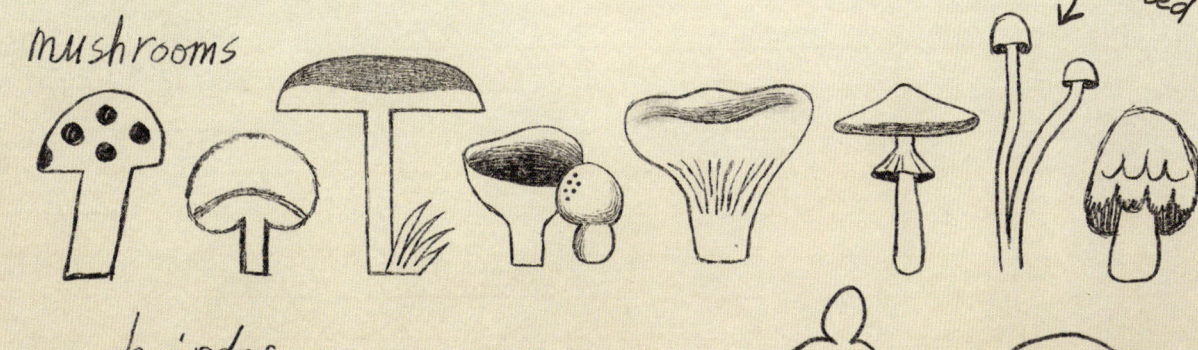

some series I've tried ↓

mushrooms

hairdos

Spend the first day collecting images or books to reference so that you have a pile of specific examples ready.

silly shoes ↓

EXERCISES

ARTISTIC ENDURANCE:

SPEND THIRTY DAYS ON JUST ONE SUBJECT. SEE HOW DEEP YOU CAN GET INTO THE DETAILS.

Best wishes on your scribbled journeys ahead —

don't forget to take wiggle-breaks and baby donkey intermissions!

L & C HARDTMUTH
300/60
TRADE MARK SINCE 1896
Made in Germany
Polychromos
FABER-CASTELL